# 1. CHRIST, THOU ART M
## (Christus, der ist mein Leben)

Violin 2

J.S. BACH

RICHARD E. THURSTON

B484

# 2. I WILL NOT LEAVE THEE, JESUS
## (Meinen Jesum lass' ich nicht)

# 3. CHRIST THE LORD, GOD'S ONLY SON
## (Herr Christ, der ein'ge Gott's Sohn)

# 4. O LORD, MY GOD
## (Ach Gott und Herr)

# 5. SURELY HIS TIME HAS COME
## (Es ist gewisslich an der Zeit)

# 6. THE NIGHT HAS COME
## (Die Nacht ist kommen)

# 7. OUR FATHER, WHO ART IN HEAVEN
### (Vater unser im Himmelreich)

# 8. SING UNTO THE LORD A NEW SONG
### (Singt dem Herrn ein neues Lied)

# 9. COME, SAVIOUR OF THE HEATHEN
### (Nun komm, der Heiden Heiland)

# 10. SLEEPERS WAKE!
### (Wachet auf!)

# 11. A CHILD IS BORN IN BETHLEHEM
### (Puer natus in Bethlehem)

# 12a. THE SON OF GOD HAS COME
### (Gottes Sohn ist kommen)

# 12b. THE SON OF GOD HAS COME
### (Gottes Sohn ist kommen)

# 16. THIS NEWBORN BABE
**(Das neugeborne Kindelein)**

# 17. CHRIST LAY IN THE BONDS OF DEATH
**(Christ lag in Todesbanden)**

# 18a. O SACRED HEAD NOW WOUNDED
### (O Haupt voll Blut und Wunden)

# 18b. O SACRED HEAD NOW WOUNDED
### (O Haupt voll Blut und Wunden)

# 19. CHRIST IS RISEN
### (Christ ist erstanden)

# 20. BY THE WATERS OF BABYLON
## (An Wasserflüssen Babylon)

# 21. FROM MY SOUL'S DEPTHS I CRY TO THEE
## (Aus tiefer Noth schrei' ich zu dir)

## 22. TO THEE ALONE, LORD JESUS CHRIST
### (Allein zu dir, Herr Jesu Christ)

## 23. A MIGHTY FORTRESS IS OUR GOD
### (Ein' feste Burg ist unser Gott)

# 24. NOW THANK WE ALL OUR GOD
### (Nun danket alle Gott)

# 25. JESU, PRICELESS TREASURE
### (Jesu, meine Freude)

# 26. O MAN, BEWAIL THY GREVIOUS SIN
### (O Mensch, bewein' dein' Sünde gross)

# 27. I CALL ON THEE, LORD JESUS CHRIST
### (Ich ruf' zu dir, Herr Jesu Christ)

# 28. WE ALL BELIEVE IN ONE GOD
### (Wir glauben all' an einen Gott)